Double Bubble Trouble!

Judy Bradbury

Illustrations by Cathy Trachok

LEARNING TRIANGLE PRESS
An imprint of McGraw-Hill

New York   San Francisco   Washington, D.C.   Auckland   Bogotá   Caracas
Lisbon   London   Madrid   Mexico City   Milan   Montreal   New Delhi
San Juan   Singapore   Sydney   Tokyo   Toronto

For Kelsey, the best gift God ever gave to me

McGraw-Hill

A Division of The **McGraw·Hill** Companies

1 2 3 4 5 6 7 8 9   KPT/KPT   9 0 2 1 0 9 8 7

ISBN 0-07-007040-7

McGraw-Hill books are available at special quantity discounts to use as premiums and sales promotions.
For more information, please write to the Director of Special Sales, McGraw-Hill, 11 West 19th Street, New York, NY 10011. Or contact your local bookstore.

Product or brand names used in this book may be trade names or trademarks. Where we believe that there may be proprietary claims to such trade names or trademarks, the name has been used with an initial capital or it has been capitalized in the style used by the name claimant. Regardless of the capitalization used, all such names have been used in an editorial manner without any intent to convey endorsement of or other affiliation with the name claimant. Neither the author nor the publisher intends to express any judgment as to the validity or legal status of any such proprietary claims.

Acquisitions editor: Judith Terrill-Breuer
Teacher review: Sharon Hixon
Production team: DTP computer artist supervisor: Tess Raynor
                 DTP computer artist: Charles Burkhour
Designer: Jaclyn J. Boone

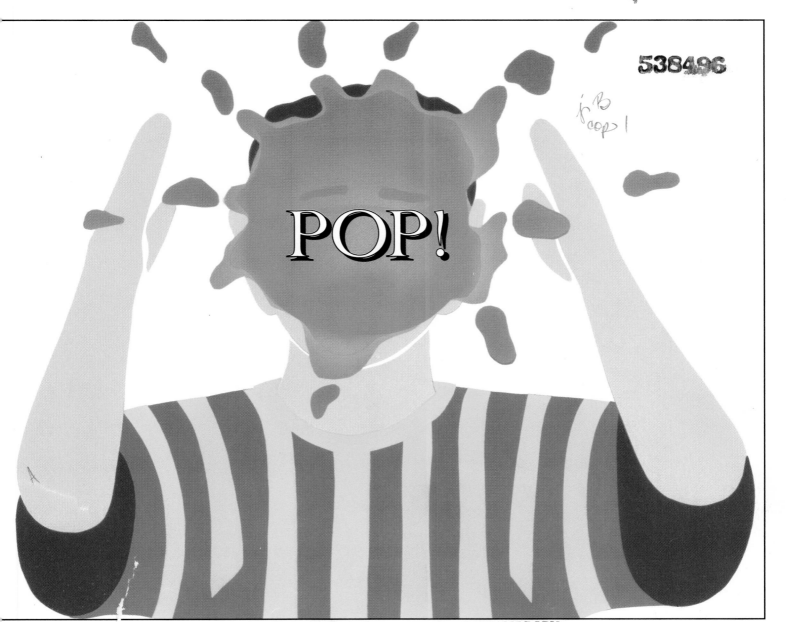

POP!

1

The floor shook as Ms. Maldonado marched down the aisle.

"Is that bubble gum all over your face?" Her eyes were enormous behind her glasses.

Christopher fingered the sticky film clinging to his cheeks, his nose, his eyebrows.

"I guess so," he answered.

"Did you bring enough for everyone?"

"N-n-no," Christopher stammered.

"Then put it here." Ms. Maldonado held out the waste
basket. Whopping Watermelon Wonder, red and rubbery and
full of flavor, landed on a mass of tissues and pencil shavings.
Most of it, that is. The rest stayed on Christopher's face.

COLORS

6

Ms. Maldonado returned to the board.

"When you have lots of things to count," she said, "it's quicker if you count by twos. 2-4-6-8 . . ."

Christopher tried to concentrate, but his eyebrows felt glued to his forehead.

Finally it was time to go home. "Line up, two by two," said Ms. Maldonado. Suddenly Christopher had an idea. He smiled and strands of bubble gum tugged at his cheeks.

Christopher counted his classmates, starting with himself. "1-2-3 . . ." Then he remembered. Counting by twos was quicker. "2-4-6-8-10-12-14-16-18-20. Rachel is absent, so one more makes 21. But I think I'll get 22." Christopher giggled. "Now I can't wait until tomorrow!" he said.

Christopher headed straight to the corner store.

"22 pieces of today's special, please," he said.
The gum clinging to his cheeks felt funny when he talked.

Mr. Skipworth chuckled. He tipped the jumbo jar
and out tumbled a pile of Power Bubble.

"This makes double the bubbles," he said, and counted
the gum two by two. "That will be 22 cents, please."

1 2 3 4 5 6 7
8 9 10 11 12 13 14
15 16 17 18 19 20 21
22 23 24 25 26 27 28
29 30

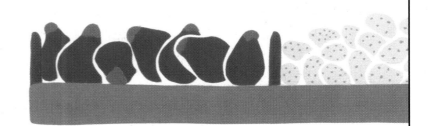

Specials Today!
1¢ each

VEGET

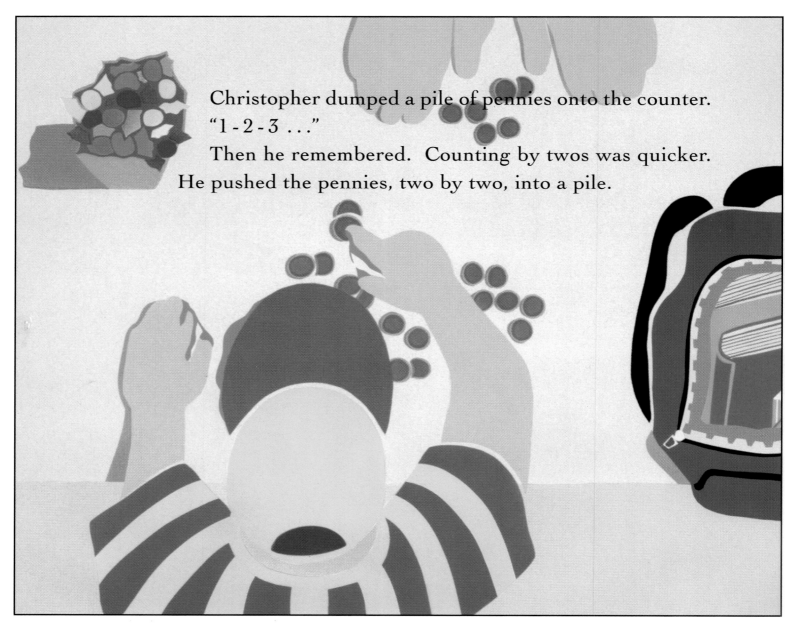

Christopher dumped a pile of pennies onto the counter.
"1 - 2 - 3 . . ."
Then he remembered. Counting by twos was quicker.
He pushed the pennies, two by two, into a pile.

Christopher tossed the bag of bubble gum into his backpack.

"Thanks!" he said and stepped outside.

Suddenly, Doofus, a one-hundred-pound Saint Bernard puppy, rounded the corner, his leash flying. Christopher jumped back just in time.

"Hah! Missed me!" he called out. He adjusted his visor and felt icky, sticky gum glued to his cap.

Christopher was at the end of the block before he realized he was being followed.

"You dropped something," said one of the girls. She pointed to the trail of gum that had fallen out of Christopher's backpack. The other girl looked at his face and giggled.

Christopher laughed, too. "Want some?" he asked.

"Cool!" they exclaimed in unison.

Christopher brushed off a piece of gum for each of them.

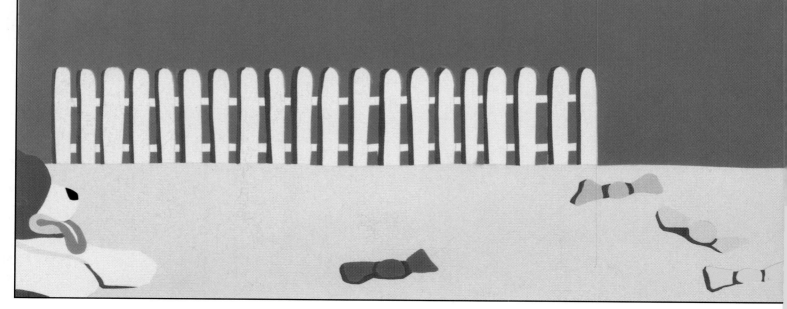

Just as the girls wheeled away, Doofus returned. He sniffed. He snuffled. He spotted the gum. Christopher dove, but Doofus was quicker.

He grabbed a mouthful of Power Bubble, wrappers and all, and galloped off.

"Watch out for your eyebrows!" Christopher yelled.

He counted his gum. Sixteen pieces. He needed twenty-two. Christopher counted on his fingers. "17-18-19-20-21-22." I hope I have enough money, he thought. Then he went back for six more pieces of gum.

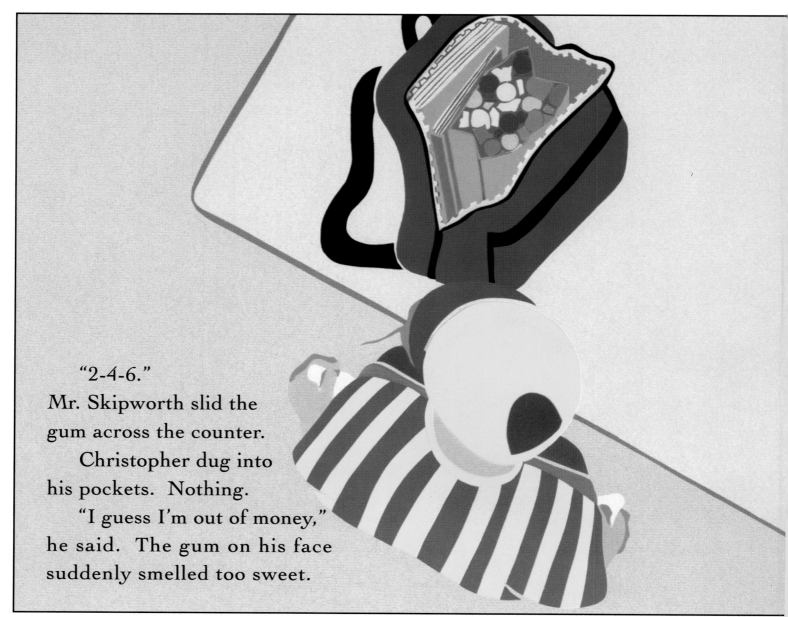

"2-4-6."
Mr. Skipworth slid the
gum across the counter.
Christopher dug into
his pockets. Nothing.
"I guess I'm out of money,"
he said. The gum on his face
suddenly smelled too sweet.

"That's okay," said Mr. Skipworth. "These bubbles are on me."
"Wow!" said Christopher. "Thanks!" This time he zipped his
backpack all the way.

When he got home, Christopher found Anthony scrubbing dried egg yolk from the carpet in his car. As Christopher slid onto the front seat, he caught a glimpse of himself in the rear view mirror.

Thin red strings fanned across his face. When he tried to brush them away, they clumped together. The more he rubbed, the stickier he got.

Without thinking, he wiped his hands on the seat.

Uh-oh, he thought.
"Does that cleaner take
off sticky stuff?" he asked.

"Why?" Anthony looked up, banging his head on the dashboard. Christopher reached into his backpack. "How about a piece of gum?" he offered. "In fact, take two," he said, scooting out of the car.

In the kitchen, Mom was working on the computer.

"I'm home," Christopher called out.

But not for long, he thought. Now he'd have to go back and buy two more pieces of bubble gum. Christopher glanced at the clock. Two hours until Mr. Skipworth's store closed.

Then he remembered he had no money.

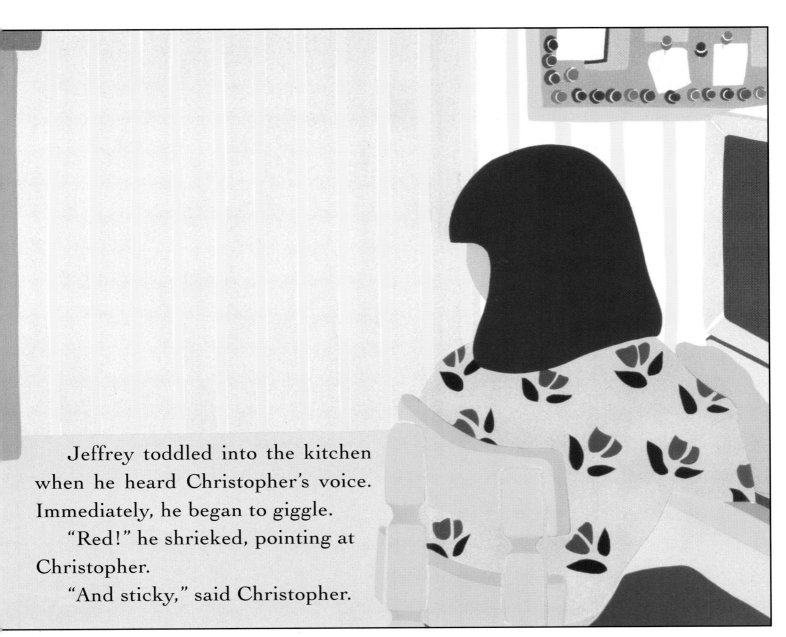

Jeffrey toddled into the kitchen
when he heard Christopher's voice.
Immediately, he began to giggle.

"Red!" he shrieked, pointing at
Christopher.

"And sticky," said Christopher.

Mom smiled. She reached for the
jar of peanut butter, knelt down, and
dabbed at Christopher's face.

"That must have been some bubble," she said.

Christopher grinned. "Even Ms. Maldonado was impressed."

Meanwhile, Jeffrey lifted the bag of bubble gum from his brother's backpack and slid under the table.

"Yum! Gum!" Jeffrey slobbered.

"That's *my* gum!" cried Christopher.
"Gum?" Mom said. "Don't swallow it!"

Jeffrey looked up, his eyes wide, his cheeks full, his mouth a mass of gooey gum.

Christopher had to laugh. Then he reached inside the bag and gave two pieces of gum to his mother. Nobody loved bubble gum more than Mom.

"Save these for after dinner," Christopher joked.

"I can always count on you to think of others," said Mom.

He counted his gum.
14 pieces. Then he counted
on his fingers. "15-16-17-
18-19-20-21-22."
He needed 8 more.
"Mom," he said, "may
I have 8 cents?"
"Why, Christopher?"
"It's a secret. But I can
tell *you*."

The next morning Christopher stashed the bag of Power Bubble in his desk. He would wait for just the right moment.

"Good morning," said Mrs. Maldonado.

"Today, let's count by twos, beginning with the number one."

"That's *odd*," Carmella said.

Ms. Maldonado laughed. "Would you like to begin?"

"1-3-5-7-9." Carmella swung her pigtails.

This was the moment!

Christopher slipped a piece of Power Bubble into his mouth.

"Rachel, what comes next?" asked Ms. Maldonado.

"Eleven?" Rachel answered.

"That's right." Ms. Maldonado was just about to turn to the board when . . .

40

POP!

Ms. Maldonado stared at Christopher.

"Bubble gum? Again?" Her voice rose with each word.

"Yes," Christopher admitted.

"Did you bring enough for everyone?" she asked.

Christopher whipped the bag of bubble gum
out of his desk.

"Power Bubble!" exclaimed Ms. Maldonado.
"That makes double the bubbles!"

Christopher handed a piece of gum to each of his classmates.

"That's 21," he said, walking up to Ms. Maldonado. "And one for you makes 22." Everyone laughed.

Except Ms. Maldonado.

Discoveries You can read this story, and you can count it, too!

Count by twos as high as you can.
- Can you count the crayons on page 6 by twos?

What shapes do you see on pages 10 and 11?
- *Hint:* If you need help, look at
  Ms. Maldonado's board on page 3.

Look at the calendar on pages 12 and 13.
- What month do you think it might be? Why?
- If you wanted to buy 3 candy canes,
  how much money would you need?
- How much money would you need if
  you decided to buy *all* the candy canes?
- Count the vegetables.
  What is there the most of?

How much gum did Doofus get on pages 20 and 21?
- *Hint:* Don't forget that Christopher
  gave a piece to each of the girls!

Look at the pictures on pages 26 and 27.
- How much gum does Christopher have
  after he gives Anthony two pieces?

Look at the pictures on pages 28 and 29.
- What time does Mr. Skipworth's store close?
  How do you know?

POP!

"Count up" with Christopher on pages 36 and 37.
- He has 14 pieces of gum. He needs 22.
  "Count up" on your fingers beginning with
  the number 15 just like Christopher does!
- Tricky math! How much gum did Jeffrey get?
  (*Hint:* Remember, Anthony and Mom each
  got two pieces.)

On page 39, Carmella makes a joke.
- What is it?
- *Hint:* When you count 2-4-6-8-10,
  you are using *even* numbers.